Forward

The book series "The Adventures of Mimi the Bulldog" are based on the life experiences and events of Mimi Marie Escalante, an English bulldog from Downey, California. Mimi was born on June 6, 2015 and arrived at her new home on July 23, 2015.   Mimi immediately transformed the hearts of her family. The series portrays Mimi's kindness, love, wittiness, free spirit and at times her mischievous behavior. Most importantly each story attempts to leave a morale or a life lesson to children and their families, a message of love. Mimi's mission and purpose is to make others happy and through her stories she is attempting to foster the bond among family. Mimi is undergoing obedience training to become a Therapy dog at a local children's hospital and reading program.

Dedication

This book series is dedicated to my family; my mother, grandmother, belated grandfather, and belated great aunt, who were my foundation from a young age. They provided such a loving and healthy upbringing. The values, morals and traditions they instilled in me define who I am today. This book would not be possible without the support of my husband. My husband who inspires me to be a better person each day, to dream, to have a vision and take action. He brought Mimi into our lives and supported me in all my ideas. I also dedicate this book to all the families in the world because family is everything and our love and bond should be fostered every single day. Finally but not least, I dedicate this story to my little Mimi who changed my life forever, my love and my healer. She came to our lives in such a perfect time. I had no idea how she would change my life! Love conquers all!

Acknowledgements

First and foremost, I thank God for the gift of life and all the blessings I have experienced. I thank my entire family and friends who always supported me and believed in me. A special thanks to my sister-in law Maira, aunt Margarita, Lil Alex, Denise, and Diana, who have helped me take care of Mimi and helped me decorate for her parties. Also, a special thanks to my friend Paola for her constructive feedback. Thank you so much!

Dear Parents, Teachers, and/or Caregivers,

The following are some suggestions to consider to help increase your child's reading comprehension and critical thinking skills.

Before Reading the Book

- Preview the book and ask the child to identify the front of the book, the back of the book, the spine of the book.
- Identify the title of the book, and cover page.
- Establish purpose for reading.
- What do you predict the story will be about?

During Reading

- Tell me a time you felt like Mimi, a little scared, a little shy, and a little worried. How did you overcome that feeling?
  (Refer to page 6 of the book).
- Tell me a time you felt safe like Mimi. How did it feel? Who made you feel safe?
  (Refer to page 7 of the book).
- What is your favorite toy and why? (Refer to page 8 of the book).
- Why do you think so many people and children wanted to come visit Mimi and play with her?
- How do you think Mimi's family will celebrate her? (Refer to page 12 of the book).
- Tell me a time when you felt celebrated by your family and friends.

After Reading

- What did you learn from Mimi's story?
- What do you think was the main idea of the story?
- What was your favorite part of the story and why?
- What was your least favorite part of the story and why?
- Would you change the ending of the story? If so, how would you change the ending of the story?
- Tell me a time when you made someone feel welcomed and loved.

"Mimi was love, and love was Mimi...

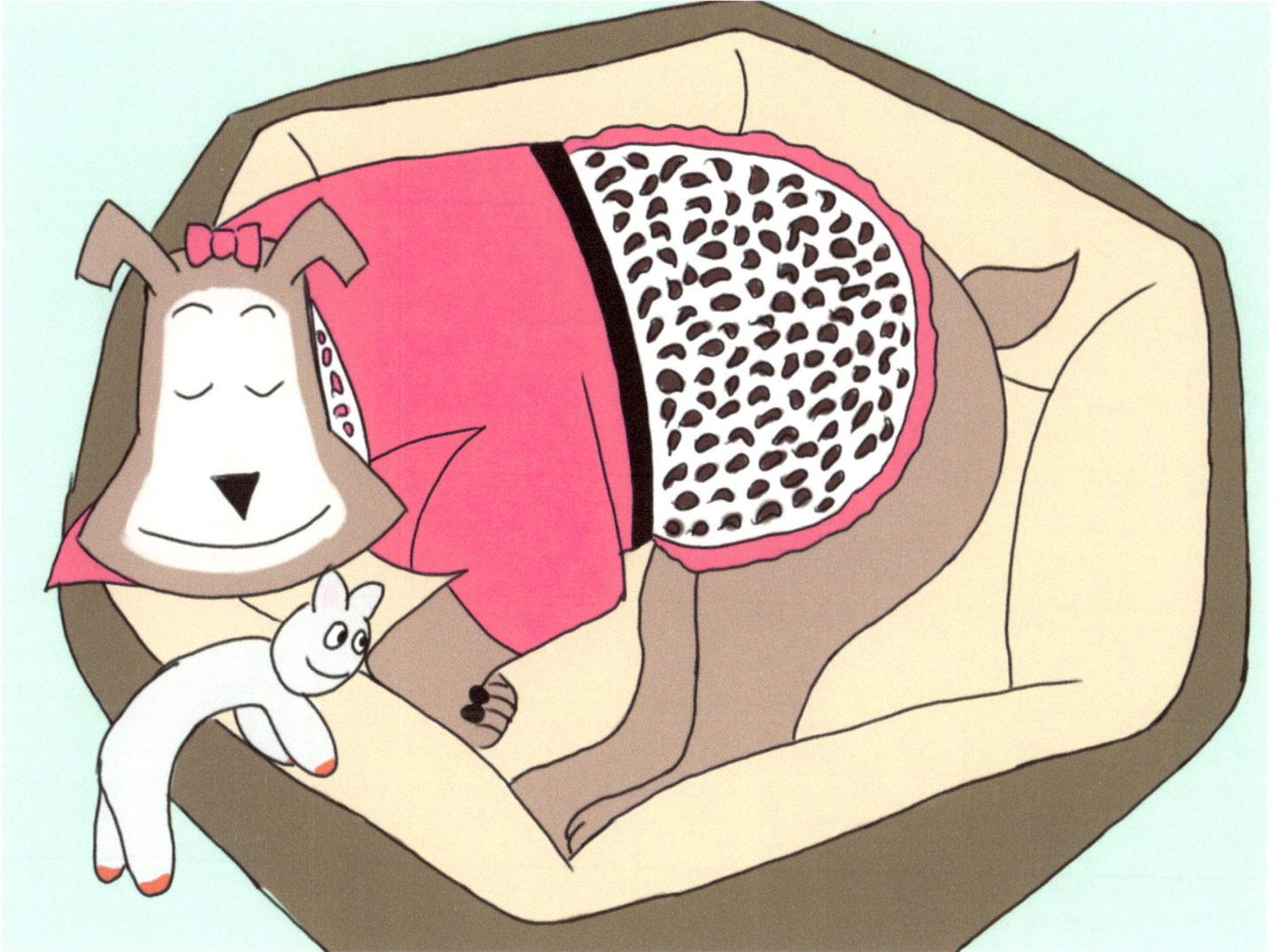

and EVERYONE became MIMIFIED!"

There she was the most beautiful, wrinkled, fluffy puppy of them all. "Mimi is here, Mimi is here!" shouted momma. Momma couldn't believe her eyes. The puppy she had always dreamed of was right in front of her. "She is too cute to be true," cried momma.

Mimi looked at her momma and then her poppa and with her big glowing eyes she sighed. Momma and poppa held Mimi in their arms, they cuddled with her and kissed her. They knew from that moment on that Mimi was special. She was no ordinary puppy but an extraordinary puppy. They felt beyond the moon, happiness, overcame their lives.

Her eyes shined bright as a diamond, her fur smooth as silk, her nails sharp as thorns, and her face cute as could be.

The very next day, Mimi woke up bright and early and started to explore her new home. She wanted to go down the stairs but she felt a little scared, a little shy, and a little worried. She started to take small steps and with the help of her momma and poppa she made it down the stairs.

She walked around the rest of the house and noticed a white and furry dog. At first she didn't know what to do, she froze! Sparky, the white dog came up to her and started licking her face. Before she knew it, they had started playing. Sparky's warm personality made Mimi feel safe.

Mimi had become quite the sensation. Everyday family and neighbors came to visit her. First came auntie with a gift basket. Then came the soccer team with toys and last momma's friend with a white lamb.

The lamb had become Mimi's favorite toy. She ran with the lamb. She pulled the lamb. She dragged the lamb and she hid the lamb. She played with the lamb in the morning, in the afternoon, and all through night time.

Mimi played with different people everyday. First she played with little Alex. They played tug of war, fetch and catch, hide and go seek, and each and every time she licked his face and wagged her little tail.

Then she played with Cyrus, who liked to squeeze her, smother her, hold her, and sleep by her side.

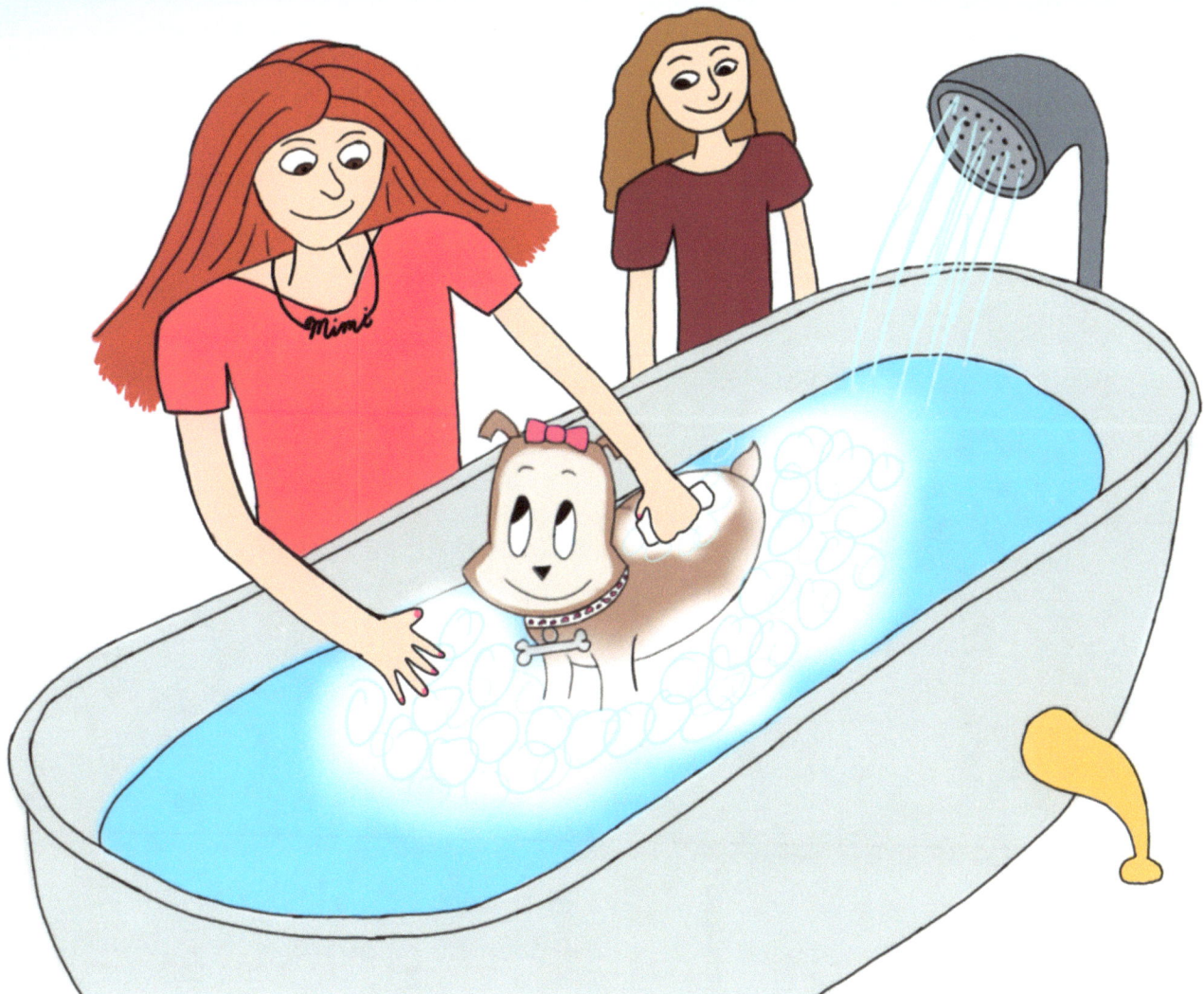

Auntie Mayra also came everyday to help bathe her, clip her nails, wash her ears, and clean her folds. She even made Mimi a pink blanket, it was warm, it was soft, and it was cozy!

Momma and Poppa were always right next to Mimi to make her feel loved and cared. "Mimi you will have the best welcome party ever" Momma said. Momma started creating a guest list, a food list, and a gift list. She wanted Mimi to feel celebrated and welcomed by the entire family. They wanted to celebrate her life! Another member of the family had been born!

Mimi's dress was pink with brown and black spots. Her collar had many sparkles. She was sweet, she was calm, and she was kind. She was everything her family had always wanted.

Mimi was so happy! Once ready, Mimi went to the backyard. She was in awe. She could not believe her eyes. It was beautiful! Mimi loved her banner filled with her pictures and balloons. The tables were decorated so colorful. Mimi had a dessert table with her name. She had a doggy table with goodie bags for all of her guests.

Family and friends started to arrive and they were all surprised with Mimi and her party. "You are such a gorgeous girl," grandma said. Mimi took a picture with each of her guests. She later danced with her momma and her poppa.

Mimi became really excited when she saw her friends, she began playing with Cookie, Sammy, Snowy and Yogi. Mimi rolled in the grass with them, she rolled in the dirt, and she rolled all the way to the pool. "Oh Gosh, Mimi fell in the pool!" screamed Momma. Poppa ran to the pool. All the dogs were soaked playing in the shallow side of the pool. "They are fine!" shouted Poppa.

Once out of the pool, Momma changed Mimi's outfit. "It's time for Mimi's cake," momma screamed. Her cake was frosty white, pink, silver and topped with her picture. All the guests had a slice of cake. "It's yummy for my tummy", said poppa. Everyone felt OVERJOYED!

Mimi had become the center of their lives, the tickle to their pickle, the light to their sadness, the apple of their eyes.

Mimi had become family. They vowed to love her everyday, kiss her every day, hug her every day, walk her everyday, hold her tight everyday, and show her unconditional love every day!

It was just like a dream, it was just like a movie, it was just like a story, it was just so surreal! Mimi was heaven sent!

Mimi's family couldn't stop singing, couldn't stop jumping, couldn't stop laughing, couldn't stop being joyous because Mimi was love and love was Mimi and everyone became MIMIFIED!

THE END

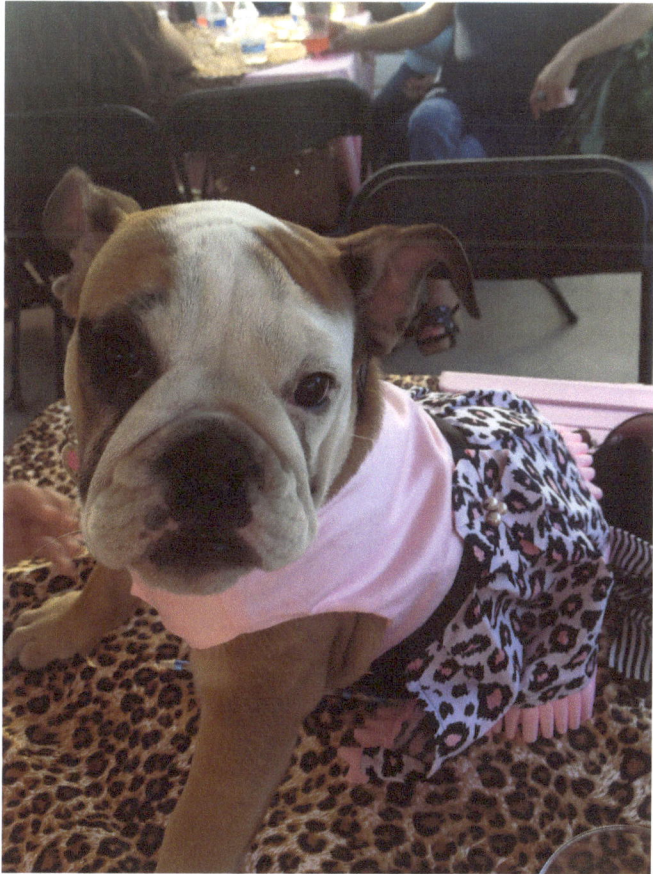

About the Author:
Dr. Donna Escalante has a doctorate degree in educational psychology from the University of Southern California. She was born and raised in South Los Angeles, California. She has worked in the field of education for over thirteen years. She has experience teaching from Kinder to college level and has conducted research and evaluation in K-12th settings, college, military, and non-profit organizations. Her mission in life is to help improve the well-being of children and their families. Through her book series she attempts to increase the literacy of children and help diminish the "word gap." The "word gap" refers to the research stating that children's vocabulary skills are linked to their economic backgrounds. By 3 years of age, there is a 30 million "word gap" between children from high and low socio-economic status. She believes "The Adventures of Mimi the Bulldog" book series can touch the lives of children and their families, strengthen their relationship, and foster love among everyone. Writing a children's book was a dream come true for Dr. Escalante. She is inspired and dedicated to take the lessons learned from Mimi, her English bulldog to a global platform. Mimi is Dr. Escalante's first dog. She believes that Mimi brought out the best in her and made her into a more patient, more loving, more empathetic, and more joyous person. Mimi was heaven sent and has transformed the lives of her entire family forever.

About the Illustrator:
Dominick Tabon is a graduate from California State University, Long Beach who majored in Film & Electronic Arts specializing in Television Production and Editing. He currently works at Long Beach State for their Live Sports Production team. His passions include Photography and sketching.

Contact Information: The audience can contact the author with any questions, comments, or inquiries via email at drescalante08@gmail.com and can follow Mimi, the English bulldog via Instagram at: Princessmimidiva